T0068219

DIET OF A CHRISTIAN

Isabell Montgomery

WESTBOW
PRESS®
A DIVISION OF THOMAS NELSON
& ZONDERVAN

WestBow Press books may be ordered through booksellers or by contacting:

WestBow Press
A Division of Thomas Nelson & Zondervan
1663 Liberty Drive
Bloomington, IN 47403
www.westbowpress.com
844-714-3454

Scripture taken from the King James Version of the Bible.

ISBN: 978-1-6642-5491-6 (sc)
ISBN: 978-1-6642-5490-9 (e)

Print information available on the last page.

WestBow Press rev. date: 02/26/2022

CONTENTS

CONTENTS

GREETINGS, AS WITH ANY ENDEAVOR WE SET OUT
TO ACCOMPLISH WE MUST FIRST ACKNOWLEDGE
THE MAKER AND CREATOR OF US ALL.

I want to praise God for so many wonderful people he has allowed to influence me along this journey. These people were on hand to ensure that I was eating on God's word for the nourishment that I would need at the time and also what I would need later in my life.

I thank my parents, Ray Pearl and Murrell Beasley.

My sisters Rita, Marilyn, Rosalind, Sharon and Denise.

My brothers Murrell Jr. and Dino.

I would especially like to thank my husband Robert, daughters Isha Ford and Uchena Spencer, grandsons Jacob and Marcus.

Withhold not thou thy tender mercies from
me, O lord; let thy loving-kindness and
thy truth continually preserve me.

Psalm 40: 11

INTRODUCTION

Well where shall I begin, on September 1998, our mother passed away from colon cancer. In the midst of our sorrow, I wanted to do something in remembrance of her legacy for her children and grandchildren.

My mother was a believer, a missionary, writer and evangelist with many gifts -- prayer being her greatest gift. She loved the Lord and His word.

Every time I looked in the mirror I saw her face; mom was all around me, in my mind and heart. I began to write and couldn't stop until the book was finished.

The pain was still there but her teachings and her life's lessons taught were now on paper.

LEVEL ONE
Becoming Christ-like

A lot of times when we diet, we think that it just affects ourselves - WRONG. The benefits from a successful diet touch others. People see the results; they ask you questions; your family notices the changes and sometimes they want to try it.

The same with your Christian diet, your growth becomes more precious to you. The promises of God you begin to feed on and you will no longer talk about how poor you are. You will lift up your head and proclaim the riches of His grace because you can't help yourself.

Level One

Important nourishment that you will need:

"Rejoice in the Lord always; and again I say, Rejoice!"

Let all your moderation be known unto men. The Lord is at hand. Be anxious for nothing, but in everything, by prayer and supplication with thanksgiving, let your requests be made known unto God. And the peace of God, which passeth all understanding, shall keep your hearts and minds through Christ Jesus." Philippians 4:-7

Remembering when I accepted the Lord as my Saviour and obtained full knowledge of accepting Him into my life, I rejoiced! I knew I had made the most important decision of my life and I was very happy. Paul, the apostle tells us to rejoice when you have made a life decision. Be happy and tell others. When most people are serious about their dieting they are not afraid to tell others. In fact, it gives them added support. Paul says, "let all know your tolerance."

Those who have just accepted the plan of salvation, made the decision to accept the scripture as the authoritative word of God, and to follow and teach God's command, then will God manifest himself in their lives. They recognize they need God and God's power.

Jesus said, "Behold, I stand at the door, and knock: if any man hear my voice, and open the door, I will come in to him, and will sup with him, and he with me" Revelation 3: 20

It's hard when you first start a diet, you feel anxious. You start eliminating favorite foods, start a new weight-loss exercise program and you need discipline. How do you stop feeling anxious? This is the first battle of the young disciple, not to worry or get distressed about the uncertain, or apprehensive about an event. When the Lord has spoken to you to do a particular task, don't feel anxious. This is the first step towards building your faith in Him, letting others see you endure and the Lord's hand at work.

Becoming anxious for nothing

In Matthew 6 verses 25-33, Jesus tells us not to be anxious about your life, what you shall eat or what you shall drink, nor about your body, what you shall put on...which of you being anxious can add one cubit to his life span? Seek first God's kingdom and His righteousness and all these things shall be yours as well.

When we have given the Lord all the praise and glory and trusted Him in all things He is pleased. For now we understand, it isn't our work but our obedience to God and His grace and mercy is what gets us into heaven.

By acknowledging God's grace and mercy, it pleases God and God blesses His children.

Once you understand first how you have been saved from condemnation and how good God has been to you, you want others to know as well. Our testimonies come from trials and tribulations. Once you start working on your diet-reading and understanding God's word, then in spite of your opposition you know you can have Victory!

Those who have just accepted the plan of salvation made a decision to accept the scripture. Election is God's choice of men and women to salvation and to service. Those who respond to God's redeeming choice enter into covenant with him. The young Christian comes to see in his own development, the love, the purpose and the plan of God for their lives. As they grow, they do not say of their own attainment "This is what I did by myself, but this is what my Father did for me". God provides the discipline and nurturing for the young Christian.

The fundamental idea in discipline is not punishment but instruction. A disciple is a learner and discipline is sound instruction. Disciples honor God and devotion towards Him.

How can we do this?

1. Paul gives us the answer "but in everything by prayer" this will be the main ingredient throughout your entire diet.

2. Another ingredient is supplication (kneeling down before God in humble submission with an earnest

heart and thanksgiving (expression of gratitude) talk to God about everything devotional quiet time to God.

You can do it or skip it but if you skip it, you not only impoverish your soul but will come short of what is expected of you when you face problems of the day.

Each young disciple must make a decision in his own heart that he will cultivate his own spiritual life by every means possible and separate from everything that would undermine or weaken that spiritual life. You will never make a success of discipleship by drifting along with the crowd because it is easy. You must take a personal stand regardless of the cost to follow the spiritual discipline necessary to make your spiritual life strong and healthy. You must separate from anything that will weaken your resolve and inter with your discipline.

The key to staying in God's word is removing those things that tempt you into sin and interferes in your prayer time and study time. What changes are you needing to make to ensure your spiritual growth?

Sometimes those obstacles are from within, but once you have been working on your diet, in spite of the opposition, you can have victory. You now have a testimony –

God has truly blessed you.

I remember my youngest daughter was attending college out of state. This was her first birthday away from home. I thought, maybe my good friend who lives in the area could take her to dinner for me. I thought maybe I could send some flowers, or ask her roommate to do something special for me .After much thought I said, I'll go myself. I flew there because I didn't want to leave it to anyone else. I wanted her to know how much I loved her and how proud I was.

God decides sometimes to do just that and lets us know how much he loves us and then he blesses us.

Remember "For God so loved the world, that he gave his only begotten Son, that whosoever believeth in him should not perish, but have everlasting life." John 3:16

Is it time for you to go to the next level? When you have started feeling "Where am I?" What does God want me to do? You're longing for more of God and it's just not enough. You already trust God's promises without seeing first and you believe in the word before anything happens. It is still a joy to be saved and filled with the Holy Ghost!

So, here we have the main ingredients for the young Christian to build on; prayer, supplication and thanksgiving.

Then Paul says… And the peace of God, which passeth all understanding, shall keep your hearts and minds through Christ Jesus." Philippians 4:-7

Level 1 Questions

1. Are you following in His footsteps?

2. Are you having difficulty surrendering to God's will?

3. Still longing for the materials of this world?

4. Are there more losses than gains?

5. Has Satan silenced you?

6. Do you feel like obeying God?

7. Are you studying the bible as a past time?

The key to staying on the diet is removing

yourself from temptation.

Next Level?

LEVEL TWO
The Discipline Christian

My oldest daughter nursed our grandson the first six months of his new life. He received all the nutrients necessary for him at that time of development as a baby. When time came for him to change or add to his nutrients for proper growth for his body and mind, he was reluctant. He eventually accepted the diet with loving people encouraging him, and more and more nutrients were added. He got upset sometimes but he eventually accepted the new diet.

So are we in our spiritual growth, as babes in Christ, mature Christians need to love and encourage the younger disciples of Christ. They need to know why it is so important to pray and study God's word. Don't give up on the young Christians, keep encouraging them.

My mother was not just my biological mother but my spiritual mentor. There was no one else that constantly encouraged me and my sisters and brothers to go to the next level. She would preach, teach and pray with us, she was a missionary and evangelist.

Each time we were in her presence she would tell us about the goodness of the Lord, the revelation she found in the word that day. She would ask us what we thought about a scripture or the Sunday school lesson, she personally ordered books for everyone, even if their church didn't use the same one because you just couldn't get enough of the word.

She wanted to know if we had read the lesson, what we thought God was saying to us through the lesson. If we had not read the lesson then we would go over the lesson. She was always praying for others and she would encourage us to pray with her. If you were sick, she would pray for you and anoint you with blessed oil. There was no way you could visit our mother and father's house without talking about the Lord or listening to the word or having to sit down and study the word. One day she said to me" Isabell, you must go to the next level! The next level to me was a commitment I was not willing to make. I knew where I was (safe). She constantly reminded me it was time to go to the next level.

This is the level Satan comes to silence you, your testimonies, your teaching and preaching, your witnessing, your singing, any action ! He wants to sideline you, put you on the inactive list, and have you wait on someone else to first tell you what to do.

Like with our diets, in the beginning we are most excited and energized. At this level, you may not see results quickly. The good that you have put inside of you is greater than the outside results. Any diet only for outward appearances, not for yourself or to be healthier, will cause you to be unable to grasp the importance of the diet. Anytime you're just attending church, praying, singing without the power of the Holy Spirit, it's just outward appearances!

Once the miracles seem to have stopped, we tend to stop telling people about how good God is and we start doubting our salvation, God, the preacher, everything and everyone. When trials and trouble come, we separate ourselves from God and His people. Satan has done a great job in silencing us, but we must be seasoned disciples. We must know all things work for the good of those who love the Lord and in spite of our situation we can still tell others about God's goodness.

The fact that He is keeping you in the midst of your storm. What is happening is the depth of your faith is working, through the good times and the bad times continue to praise, worship, pray, study God's word and obey. You will have the faith that God intended for you.

Have you ever been in a Storm?

It was so bad that you couldn't see past the windshield.

You wondered should I stop and let it pass

You didn't know what was behind you so you kept

going. You also didn't know what was ahead of you

so you drove by faith.

After traveling for a long time in the storm you think

you see some relief

but the thunder roars and the lightning cracks and

you are frightened .

You wonder, What should I do?

Your whole body shutters you wonder

Which is worst the storm, the thunder or the

Lightning?

We have all experienced a storm, most of the time it

is unexpectedly.

Sometimes we have no warning.

Sometimes there is nothing we can do but weather

the storm.

The storm doesn't get easy but knowing you survived the last one helps.

I've been in the storm, it lasted a long time for me.

The lightning cracked and the thunder roared over, and over and over.

When you've gone through a storm you need to rebuild your faith, knowing that things will not be the same.

You will miss what you lost in the storm.

Each day is a reminder of all that was taken will be restored in eternity.

The storm pushes you to the next level of your diet on God's word and your faith.

Your recovery is totally dependent upon what you"re feeding upon.

God's promises helps you to renew yourself, not just repair, paste or pretend to be fixed.

God's word renews our minds and body.

We must feast on the promises of God. Our minds will eventually show lack of nutrients that are important. God's word heals; it gives prosperity, hope, peace, and joy. It restores love. It allows you to stand and be strong.

Job went through the storm and his faith was even more increased and he went to the next level. Peter denied Jesus three times; afterwards, he felt ashamed but Jesus forgave him and he did miraculous work at the next level.

Challenge yourself to get back into God's army. Bring those vessels to God and let God fill the vessels. Faith begins where the will of God is known. Listen to God's still voice, get into the word, pray, fellowship with God become a mighty warrior, be determined doing all God has said for you to do. Stand and see God's deliverance, do not fear, establish yourself in righteousness.

The test for success is at this level

When the disciples disputed over the question as to who should be the greatest, Jesus pointed to the world with it's selfish measures of success. "But it shall be among you" he declared, "whosoever will be great amongst you let him minister and whosoever will be chief among you, let him be your servant."

Then He pointed to Himself as the example "Even as the Son of man came not to be ministered unto, but to minister, and to give a ransom for many." Matthew 20:28

The love in which Paul speaks in I Corinthians 13 is the very essence of true religion. Without the grace of Christian love, which is greater than all spiritual gifts, the exercise of our abilities even in church and mission work is of little value in the sight of God.

When you are in a comfortable place and it is easy to do the Lord's work then you are no longer working. Jesus walked the earth doing the impossible, touching, healing, reaching, teaching, feeding, forgiving and much, much more. His work was not easy. Jesus asked His Father to let His will be done. If as a disciple we have developed a comfortable lifestyle then we have ceased to do the work of the Lord. We are no longer sacrificing ourselves. God loves for us to do the impossible. That's when miracles occur and we get a glimpse of God's awesomeness!

If there is one reason why it is causing you so much of a problem, it can be traced to the last thing a person wants to do or give to anybody, it's their will. As we know, that there is no conversion until you are willing to get on your knees before God and surrender the whole heart and life to Jesus Christ as Saviour and Lord.

This is the missionary trail that has been followed by Paul and all those who have followed in his footsteps. This is where our work begins with the diet. We can rest assured that if we, day by day, faithfully labor and witness in the place where God has put us, He will always be with us.

When a person says he is a disciple, yet he does nothing about the lost souls around him, has he surrendered to the Lord Jesus? When we become true disciples by receiving the Lord Jesus who is presented to us through the preaching of the gospel from the word of God, we receive Him and have an everlasting life. God says take on the burden yourself, stand in the gap for a person until God does the work. Intensity of prayer in warfare when facing warfare makes your prayer so intense, the storm on the outside will not harm the ship, only when the storm get in the inside will the ship sink. Unbelief inside.

As we labor, we will find like Paul when came down to the end of his ministry, he found himself in a Roman jail with no companion save the One who was with him all the way through, and who never left him. That was the fulfillment of the promises the Lord Jesus gave in the command that if we obey the great commission He will always be with us.

When Paul was standing in the shadow of martyrdom, it was not the end of the trail but the triumphant entrance into a new field of recognition of service.

It's not until we have advanced in the Christian life that we realize the heights of conduct God intended for us. Sin severed and separated us from God and His plan for us. Must sin always harass and frustrate us at every turn?

No, for the bible echoes back " Behold the Lamb of God who taketh away the sins of the world." John 1:29

Christ died for our sins, Christ has dealt with sin on the cross, rose a mighty conqueror over sin and death. He lives and desires to enter man's heart with dynamic salvation imparting to your life a realization of God's purpose and destiny for you now and for eternity in Heaven.

Again, if you don't study, pray and obey so shall we die for lack of nourishment . It is important to receive the correct diet that is sufficient for your Christian journey that you will not faint but rise like an eagle. For the race is not given to the swift but to those who endure to the end.

Some days or weeks before my mother went to sleep on earth to spend eternality with the Lord, she told me very excitedly, "Isabell, I have such a peace, I just can't describe it to you."

This was right in the midst of her losing battle with cancer. It had taken a complete toll on her body but not her spiritual soul. She had already lost weight and was unrecognizable even to herself. She had constant pain and knowing her days here on earth was numbered she still able to say " I have such a peace".

"Yea doubtless, and I count all things but loss for the excellency of the knowledge of Christ Jesus, my lord; for whom I have suffered the loss of all things, and do count them but refuse, that I may win Christ

And be found in him not having mine own righteousness, which is of law, but that which is through the faith of Christ, the righteousness which is of God by faith;

That I may know him, and the power of his resurrection, and the fellowship of his sufferings, being made conformable unto his death. Philippians 3: 8-10

It is important to make the necessary adjustments as we reach the different levels of our christian journey. If you are on the wrong diet you cannot operate on the level that God would have you to be. Your knowledge of who God is and His works and power has to operate in different levels of your faith. As we grow so should our faith and power in God.

Dedication to Mrs. Ray Pearl Beasley

Thanks Mom for showing us
How awesome God's love is
You saw in your family and others
What we were capable of becoming
You wouldn't allow us to give up on ourselves or others
Because you never gave up on us

When we needed that special touch you were there
We learned that we had a responsibility to
Love one another
We thank God for your life and the footsteps
You left behind
You were a solider in the army of the Lord
You told us to try your "Jesus, He's alright"
Your testimony was you loved to call on the name Jesus
You talked about "His saving power, His healing and
His forgiving power
We look forward with great anticipation when we can
All be together
What a day of rejoicing that will be!

Written September 1999 by Isabell Montgomery

Study Pray and Obey

1. Do you really know God's word and God's power?

2. Is your prayer " bread of heaven feed me until I want
   no more?

3. Do you need the water where you will thirst no more?

4. Do you need your soul restored, with your cup running
   over?

Next Level?

Fear knocked at the door, Faith answered

No one was there.

LEVEL THREE
God's Servant

In April 1998, the doctor told my mother that she had cancer and it was bad, without surgery she would surely die. Fear knocked at the door, faith answered, there was no one there. For she is weak but He is strong.

Most people tend to put the focus on human body as being all, but the spirit man is more powerful of them all. The Holy Spirit manifest itself greatly when the human body becomes weak.

For she is weak but He is strong.

The human body is limited to time and goes back to the earth but the Spirit man time is endless. Only God gives us time,

time limits the human body parts and functions. The spirit man was never intended to live on earth.

For she is weak but He is strong.

The Holy Spirit is a reminder of what is to come in our heavenly home and we will never be alone.
For she is weak but He is strong

The Holy Spirit doesn't comply with scientific data for the human body- it dwells in the shell of the human body it is not a part of the flesh it do supernatural -miraculous things
For she is weak but He is strong

The body parts are dependent upon each one to function properly in order to live. The Holy Spirit is God all by Himself (God the Father, the Son and the Holy Spirit)
For she is weak but He is strong

And while the fleshly man whispers the doom conditions of the human body- the Holy Spirit rises up and says respect me for Greater is I than the flesh that's in the earth

For she is weak but He is strong

My Mom told me with such urgency and sternness "you can't stay where you are, you must go to God's next level he has for you." In other words grow in your walk otherwise you will not be able to weather the storm.

I recognize the magnitude of what I had lost a spiritual teacher, disciplinary, and motivator. I cried and cried until there were no more tears. The natural breathing function stopped. She was gone in my mind at the time. I thought of her boarding the Ole ship of Zion. I didn't know where it was, where it was going or the destination. She was on that ship, that's all I could picture in my head. A place I couldn't see or know.

So much pain, too much pain, everything inside of me in pain - breathe. I had lost the ability to breathe, as I grasped for breath my daughter screamed " Mom, Breathe!"

God was so good to his servant before mother left here we were her children- a younger daughter who aspire to be all

God has in store, another daughter who sang like an angel with such anointing power, her other daughters with love for the Lord and me. The one she was constantly admonishing to take my walk with the lord to the next level.

Don't stay where you are, there's so much more, my mother who wanted all the gifts God had for his people, speaking in tongues, and interpretations, casting out devils, teaching and going into the fields with the gospel. Here we were surrounding her, speaking in tongues and anointing her body with her blessed oil as she had done us, kneeling by her side praying, my sister singing God's praise.

I felt God was speaking to her, giving her confirmation regarding her children and preparation for us surely she knew God was using even me. Was God telling her I would rise to the next level, that all her daughters would go to the next level?

Was God telling me I would rise to the next level?

One of the greatest results of the coming power at Pentecost was the new attitude of the disciples toward their possession. The power that came upon them was strong enough to conquer covetousness, they thought of themselves as channels of divine blessing at the command of Christ. All they were and all they possessed they held ready for the Master's use.

What does our religion cost us? When someone says he is a Christian yet does nothing about lost souls around him, do you feel his religion can mean very much to him? Usually we get out of it just what we put into it. We find little joy in our Christian experience if we do not work at it. It is a full-time experience, a seven days a week job to be a christian. Most of us do not know the joy of our faith because we have not paid the price. A price that involves unconditional surrender of self to the Lord Jesus.

I never saw a useful disciple who was not a student of the bible. If a man neglects the bible he may pray and ask God to use him, but there is not much for Holy Spirit to work with. We must have the word itself. The word is sharper than a two edged sword. People may say we want something new but if you get tired of the word of God and it becomes wearisome to you, you are out of communion with God. What you need is someone who will unfold and expound God's word to you. The older you grow the more precious it will become to you!

Then take the promises of God. Let a man feed for a month on the promises of God and he will not talk about how poor he is. He will lift his head up and proclaim the riches of His grace because he could not help doing it.

Spend time in prayer, then take up hope, faith, grace, mercy and feed on them. The bible will become a new book to you.

"God is our refuge and strength, a very present help in trouble. Therefore, we will not fear though the earth be removed, and though the mountains be carried into the midst of the sea."

Psalm 46:1-2

Christians that have been in church for many years, participating but have now become sluggish, always complaining, no longer rejoicing, no testimonies- wrong diet. You need a more effective, more victorious diet for discipleship.

I'm a solider in the army of the Lord. Challenge yourself to get back into God's army. Bring those vessels to God and let God fill the vessels.

Be determined, doing all God has said for you to do. Listen to God's still voice. Fellowship with God. Become a mighty warrior. See God's deliverance. Establish yourself in righteous

Your growth becomes more precious to you. The promises of God you begin to feed on, you will no longer talk about how poor you are, you will lift up your head and proclaim the riches of His grace because you can't help yourself.

When we become true disciples by receiving Jesus we have everlasting life and God sets us apart for a work of ministry for Him. When we come to the place we are willing to present ourselves to the Lord, holding nothing back, He will then reveal to us His will concerning our service.

The Lord is my shepherd, I shall not want. He makes me lie down in green pastures, He leads me beside the still waters, He restores my soul, He leadeth me in the paths of righteousness for his name's sake. Psalm 23:1-3

Paul left this triumphant testimony "I have fought a good fight, I have finished my course, I have kept the faith; Henceforth, there is laid up for me a crown of righteousness, which the Lord, the righteous judge, shall give me in that day, and not to me only but unto all them also that love His appearing" II Timothy 4:7-8

I eventually made that commitment to the next level. I started feeling the anointing on my life, I studied God's word with a passion. I was eager to go see my father at my parent's house to discuss the word! Then another storm arose, my father sitting at the dinner table with his food set aside (feasting on the word of God) tells us he was leaving to get some rest just like our Mother.

At that time the word needed to be real to all of us. He had made his mind up he was going to get some rest. I knew God's promises but the pain was still there. This time with great anticipation I looked forward to seeing them.

When we all get together "What a day of rejoicing that will be!"

God says " For I will pour water upon him that is thirsty, and floods upon the dry ground; I will pour my Spirit upon their seed, and my blessing upon thine offspring" Isaiah 44:3

Next Level?

LEVEL FOUR
Holy and Sanctified

"Yea, though I walk through the valley of the shadow of death, I will fear no evil; for thou art with me; thy rod and thy staff they comfort me." Psalms 23:4

Having to process the news that my father gave me, I was feeling very confused and empty, what I was dieting on wasn't enough for my survival. It was time for a change. Apparently the diet had not achieved the desired outcome.

It may have been comfortable and familiar to remain but a subtle nudging or a whisper encouraging me to move beyond and above.

As the world reflects constant change and evolution you too

must evolve. When of yourself you can do no more, you must instantly allow the Holy Spirit of God to fill you with His Presence.

If I had not decided to go to the next level my existence here on earth, I believe, would be shortened or powerless. My sister and brother went to be with our parents in glory.

It was so much pain, but my soul is alight with fire of the Holy Spirit! I stand firm with God, I know with unwavering faith that He Who is in me is greater than whatever I may face. I can because God can!

Again, if we don't study, pray and obey so shall we die for lack of nourishment. It is important to receive the correct diet and grow on your Christian journey that you will not faint but rise like and eagle!

I am thankful for the countless blessings God is ceaselessly bestowing upon me. His never-ending grace sustains, encourages and inspires me to express more of His goodness.

It may be easy to overlook the grace of God, or take it for granted. He always provides and protects without us realizing the full extent of His presence.

I know that I have the strength of God inside of me. I have feasted on the word of God. I have strength to overcome any seeming obstacles, to move mountains, and reach my destination. I will reach it just like my mother, regardless of unforeseen detours that may arise.

Today I arise with a feeling of happiness shining forth from deep in my soul. I am joyful in knowing the Lord. My happiness does not depend on my career, bank account, family or friends. My happiness does not rely on material, external conditions or situations. My happiness comes from within, I am happy because I trust God as the Source of my life.

Having the right diet of prayer, supplication, and thanksgiving and having built a relationship with God. You can then have your eternal supply of joy and peace.

Remember when I said my mother told me very excitedly, "Isabell, I have such a peace, I just can't describe it to you."

Today, I emerge a new creation in Christ. I have discarded my old ways of thinking, feeling, speaking, acting and reacting. That old diet of behaviors prevented me from operating at the optimal spiritual level. Those negative behaviors kept me in and out of the " maintenance department" constantly trying to get some malfunctioning part of my life repaired.

Revive each Christian that we may all become more involved in the deliverance of lost and suffering humanity.

Anoint us afresh. Invigorate our hearts and lives with Your Spirit, Lord. May we become action-oriented for Your service.

The standard is already set by God's word. By living up to that standard, we will be winners in every areas of our lives. Where are you in your Christian walk? Or you reading the word much more as you were then? Are you struggling to go to the next levels? Do you spend more time with God now?

- Get into the Word!

- Re-examine your diet!

- Raise your level!

Printed in the United States
by Baker & Taylor Publisher Services